A LOVE FOR
THE STRANGERS

What the Bible says about loving immigrants

PUBLISHED BY
OUR WRITTEN LIVES, LLC

Our Written Lives provides publishing services to authors in various educational, religious, and human service organizations. For information, visit www.OurWrittenLives.com.

Library of Congress Cataloging-in-Publication Data
Hartman, Rachael Kathleen 1983

A Love for the Strangers: What the Bible Says About Loving Immigrants

Library of Congress Control Number: 2020935101
ISBN: 978-1-942923-39-8 (paperback)

Unless otherwise noted, Scriptures are from the King James Version, public domain.

Alternate versions used are noted, and belong to the copyright holders thereof.

A LOVE FOR THE STRANGERS

What the Bible says about loving immigrants

Rachael Kathleen Hartman

For My Friends

C♡NTENTS

♡ Chapter One ♡

A Tribute

*I pledge allegiance to the Christian flag, and to the Savior for whose
Kingdom it stands; one Savior, crucified, risen, and coming again
with life and liberty for all who believe.*

*I pledge allegiance to the flag of the United States of America,
and to the republic for which it stands, one nation under God,
indivisible, with liberty and justice for all.*

It was the year 2000. As a senior in high school, my first job was working as a coffee barista serving specialty drinks to soldiers stationed at Fort Bragg, North Carolina. It was a fun time where I felt the freedom of having my own money, a car, and almost no bills—outside of my very first cell phone, a Nokia with limited minutes.

I was excited about graduating and planned to go to Texas Bible College, but first I wanted to go on a mission trip overseas. After graduation, I went to Kenya with a group of church kids for ten days. I was 17 years old.

I have felt drawn to missionary life since I was 10 years old. I remember many instances of waking up in the middle of the night and praying for people in other countries. I was burdened in a way no one else my age seemed to be. I felt God was leading me to missions work.

That same year, age 10, was the first time God whispered to me about writing a book, but that is another story. I also met my childhood hero that year—Nona Freeman, a missionary to Africa. I loved to read her books. I admired the compassion that flowed through her as she shared testimonies of the power of God. She spoke to me directly once. I remember the kindness I felt coming from her. I cherish that memory.

When I was in 8th grade, I remember spending time praying for many different people groups. I didn't have a specific group I felt called to. I just had a love for and interest in various cultures.

A few months after my trip to Africa in 2001, I went to the prayer room of my church after work. I was alone and couldn't seem to pray through the dark heaviness I felt. The church had set up tables around the room with information and prayer guides to help people in their prayer time. I walked around to each station and stopped at the missionary table. That area was dedicated to praying for missionaries around the world. There was a book full of names and pictures of the missionaries the church financially supported.

I had brought back a soapstone egg from Kenya that was painted like a globe, and had left it on the missions table. I picked up that egg and kissed it—something I would not normally do. When I looked down, I had kissed America.

Suddenly, the Holy Spirit hit me so hard I fell to my knees interceding for our country. I could not stop crying as the Holy Spirit flowed through me for a long time. It was getting late and I was 18 years old with a curfew, so I had to go home. I went home praying because the heaviness I felt would not ease. I finally fell asleep.

The next day, I got up and dressed for work. My mom was home, sitting at the dining room table. She was listening to the news on the radio, and crying.

I was late for work, and Mom couldn't stop crying enough to explain why she was crying. She just kept shaking her head and pointing at the radio.

Looking back, I now realize she was in shock. Back then, I didn't understand. I left for work and listened to the news on my drive. Even then, I still didn't understand exactly what was happening.

I arrived at the coffee shop in the 82nd Airborne PX and began setting up for the day. The TVs were on in the PX and soldiers had gathered around them. Everyone was silent.

We were under attack. The Trade Center Towers were falling. Our whole world felt like it was crashing down.

I didn't know what to do, so I just did my job and started making coffee for the soldiers.

Two particular Special Forces soldiers would always come by the coffee shop for Mocha Java Milkshakes. One of them stopped by and ordered their regular two shakes. I asked where his friend was, and he just smiled. I never saw those two men again. I later heard that Special Forces troops deployed to the Middle East within the hour of the first plane hitting the first tower.

As the daughter of an Active Duty Army Officer, 9/11 was not only scary in the way it was for all Americans, it also meant potentially more personal sacrifice. I was afraid my dad would be sent to war. I grew up with that fear, and now it was even more real than it was in the 90s during the Gulf War when I was in third grade.

God did spare my family, and a few months later—while everyone else was put on stop-loss—my dad's retirement papers were miraculously approved, and he did not have to deploy. But several of my friends and acquaintances did deploy. Our community grieved not only for the losses that happened on 9/11, but also for the people we loved that were sent into harm's way.

I remember praying for U.S. soldiers and for their protection. I even remember naively praying for Saddam Hussein to die of a heart attack so that the conflict would end, and our soldiers could come home. As a teenager, I didn't realize how complicated the situation was.

I remember when they found Saddam Hussein, and when they pulled down the big statue of him in Baghdad. I listened to the radio broadcast of his hanging. I recall the announcement of his death not bringing me any sense of peace, but only the knowledge that death—no matter how just—did not solve anything.

I lost two friends in the war. In 2010, Sgt. Chris Stout was killed in action in Afghanistan by an enemy ambush. In 2013, Sgt. William Brown also died in Afghanistan from non-combat causes.

I had worked with Brown at Fort Polk, Louisiana. He always asked about my brother, who had recently been sentenced to 10 years in prison. Brown always told me he was praying for Jeremy.

Chris Stout was a part of my friend group at church during those good teenage days in Fayetteville. He was known for his amazing singing voice. He would always sing the beautiful song about Heaven, "I Can Only Imagine." He was married to my friend, Misty, and left behind beautiful daughters.

I will never forget the sacrifice that my friends, family, acquaintances, and the men and women of our United States Military have given. I respect the time, energy, and life they and their families give to help make our country and the world a safer place.

Thank you for your sacrifice and service. I pray the world will find peace and for all wars to end.

Chapter Two

My Strangers

Not like the brazen giant of Greek fame,
With conquering limbs astride from land to land;
Here at our sea-washed, sunset gates shall stand
A mighty woman with a torch, whose flame
Is the imprisoned lightning, and her name
Mother of Exiles. From her beacon-hand
Glows world-wide welcome; her mild eyes command
The air-bridged harbor that twin cities frame.
"Keep, ancient lands, your storied pomp!" cries she
With silent lips. "Give me your tired, your poor,
Your huddled masses yearning to breathe free,
The wretched refuse of your teeming shore.
Send these, the homeless, tempest-tost to me,
I lift my lamp beside the golden door!"

The New Colossus by Emma Lazarus
Inscribed on the Statue of Liberty

I've had a love for American immigrants and international people since I was a child. Many of my closest childhood friends were children from families that had moved to the U.S. from other countries. The trend continues in my adult friendships. I find myself naturally drawn to "transplanted people." Maybe it's because I moved a lot growing up due to my father's career as an Army Chaplain.

As I write this book, I'm actively volunteering as an English teacher working with refugees at a local apartment complex. I teach women from Afghanistan, Pakistan, Iran, Iraq, Chad, Eritrea, and Malaysia. I've learned a lot about the cultures and religions of the world, and I've developed a great love for these woman, and their home-cooked international food!

There are certain people groups I'm drawn to and work more closely with, but my heart is not limited by culture when it comes to those God has called me to serve and to love. There is a special place in my heart for the many first-generation immigrants I've met through the years. I enjoy listening to their stories and being a friend. Here are some of the people who I have shared friendship with through the years.

In middle school, I had a Russian friend. I remember how her mother's tone of voice echoed through their house as she shouted in Russian. They were genuine people just living out their lives. I remember when they set up a Christmas tree in their house with Santa Clause all over it. As self-proclaimed atheists, they called it their "New Year's Tree."

In 9th grade, I had a Sikh friend. She was beautiful with long black hair. She reached out to me because we both had the longest hair in our school. She invited me over and I had the opportunity to watch as her mother and sister wrapped up her father's uncut hair into his turban. His hair stretched halfway across the room!

While in Bible College, I became friends with a Pakistani girl about my age. I met her at the local gas station. I noticed she had a slight limp and I held the door open for her and spoke to her. She invited me over to her house, telling me she had no friends and was lonely. She lived with her sister and brother-in-law.

At their home, they told me stories of what life was like for them as upper-class members of their country. I was amazed when they said that every morning they had three servants waiting for them to wake up.

As soon as they were awake, one servant would run to make breakfast. The second would be ready to make a brand-new dress for the day. The third was on standby as a driver to take them wherever they wanted to go.

We had the chance to talk about our faith, and the women asked me questions about Jesus' healing power. I can't help but think of the scriptures that mention how we will stand before kings and rulers to testify (Psalm 119:46-47, Matthew 10:18, Proverbs 22:29). We truly don't know what caliber of people are around us until we take the time to hear their stories.

While in Bible College, I also became friends with two brothers who owned the restaurant where I worked. They were from Albania and we developed a bond that made me feel like we were siblings. A few years later, my heart broke when I learned that Sam, the only one of several brothers who had been denied amnesty due to a translation issue, had an immigration problem. The other brother, Giovanni, told me they had witnessed the murder of a democratic politician in their country, which is why the family had to flee. I advocated for Sam, even going to the Texas congressman's office in D.C., but nothing seemed to help.

Giovanni later told me that after some time in prison, Sam was sedated and put on a plane to Albania. He said as soon as the plane landed and he was escorted off, that Sam was shot on-site. I always prayed that somehow his fate was not as it had been told to me.

As a graduate student, I became friends with an Indian student who worked in the same office I did. I had the opportunity to buy him a Bible in his language. He also visited church with me—it was the first time he had ever stepped into a Christian church.

As a young professional, I became friends with a diverse group of people my age at work. Our group consisted of myself, a French woman who was a non-practicing Catholic, an atheist American, and two Muslim men—one of whom was married to a Christian preacher's daughter. We had a dinner party one night where the French woman made us rice with milk and strawberries. Our discussion was lively, and I will never forget that night.

After that, my next job led me to meet several Middle Eastern translators who were serving in the U.S. Army. Currently, as an English teacher, I have had the opportunity to become friends with many more Muslims from various countries. I've spent quite a bit of time with them and cherish our friendships. Their war-torn stories wrench my heart, and I am so proud of how far they have come since immigrating to America.

Over the years, I have had the privilege of meeting a lot of international people I've grown to love. I have also met some over the internet. For the past few years, I have been teaching English to the most precious Chinese children online. I love them dearly. I have also developed friendships with some of my local adult students' family members who still live overseas.

As my heart for people continues to grow, God fuels my passion with dreams and visions. One night a few months ago, I was standing at my bathroom sink when I had a vision. It was of a young woman that was about as tall as my shoulders. She was dressed in a black burka from head to toe. She leaned on my shoulder, hugged me, and cried. She was depressed. I don't know if the vision represented a particular woman, or many women, but I began to pray against depression.

Recently, I took my parents to observe our English class. There was a young woman in her late twenties in the class from Afghanistan. When she learned I had my mother with me, she started crying. She said she missed her mother. I hugged her and later visited her home several times.

Later, I was able to visit her in her home and hear more of her story. I know my vision of the depressed woman was preparing my heart to be open and sensitive to the needs of the people I'm working with.

These stories are just a tiny glimpse into the bonds I have formed through the years. In the final chapter, I share a few more stories of the people I've met. The rest of this book shares Biblical principles for how we treat immigrants.

The Bible has plenty to say about the way we treat the "strangers" among us. Compassion and hospitality are key virtues the Word of God commands, no matter who we encounter.

As a college student, I had the opportunity to present a paper at a small human rights conference. My topic was Immigration and the Bible. This study is based on my paper and the speech I presented at that conference.

It is my prayer that you begin to see the beauty of the lives of the people all around you, and that the Word of God will empower you to show Christ's love to the international people in your world.

Chapter Three

Biblical Words & References

One law shall be to him that is homeborn,
*and unto the **stranger** that sojourneth among you.*

Exodus 12:49

People have been immigrating long before documented history. Anthropological findings support theories of nomadic tribes moving around the world. The dictionary defines an immigrant as "a person who migrates to another country, usually for permanent residence; an organism found in a new habitat; or a plant or animal that establishes itself in an area where it previously did not exist."

The Bible has a lot to say about immigrants. The Old Testament often reminds the Israelites of their history of immigration, and how God led them out of old places and into new lands. There were also several Old Testament laws on how to treat immigrants that moved along with the children of Israel.

The Bible doesn't call immigrants "immigrants." Instead, it uses words like foreigners, aliens, sojourners, and strangers. The Bible also does not distinguish between "legal" and "illegal" immigrants the way U.S. culture often does.

In the King James Version of the Bible, immigrants are referred to as "foreigners" in four verses. They are called "aliens" in 15 verses, and "sojourners" in 72 verses.

The most common Biblical term for an immigrant is "stranger." There are 198 references to "strangers" in the King James Version of the Bible. Of those 198 verses, over 55 simply mention strangers in passing, an additional 50 verses that mention strangers are within the books of the law; 45 verses discuss the treatment of strangers and 14 verses remind Israel that they used to be "strangers" in the land.

Before we dig into the Bible characters and Biblical commands concerning the treatment of immigrants, I want to share three concepts I found interesting about the strangers of the Old Testament.

1. At times there was a language barrier. Some strangers among the Israelites spoke their language and some did not. Those who did understand, listened to the Word of God as it was read. Read Joshua 8:35.

*There was not a word of all that Moses commanded, which Joshua read not before all the congregation of Israel, with the women, and the little ones, **and the strangers that were conversant among them.***

2. The number of strangers living among the people was important to the Israelite leadership. Read 2 Chronicles 2:17.

*And Solomon **numbered all the strangers** that were in the land of Israel, after the numbering wherewith David his father had numbered them; and they were found an hundred and fifty thousand and three thousand and six hundred.*

3. Strangers often worked behind the scenes and held jobs that others found less desirable. Read Isaiah 61:5.

*And **strangers** shall stand and feed your flocks, and the **sons of the alien** shall be your plowmen and your vinedressers.*

Questions to Consider

1. What words does the Bible use to describe people we would call immigrants? How do you define the word immigrant?

2. How were the lives of Old Testament immigrants similar to the lives of immigrants in our world today?

3. What are some other words we might use to describe immigrants in our culture?

Other words we may use in English: refugee, alien, legal or illegal immigrant, migrant worker, global nomad, defector, deportee, evacuee, exile, expatriate, relocatee, repatriate, foreigner, noncitizen, nonnative, colonist, newcomer, squatter, migrator, pilgrim, pioneer, trekker, etc.

Chapter Four

Immigrants in the Bible

There is nothing new under the sun.

Ecclesiastes 1:9

We don't always have the privilege of knowing the stories behind why people immigrate to our country. We can guess they either moved for better opportunities or were forced to relocate due to war or natural disaster. The same is true for Bible characters who found themselves immigrating. Immigrants, nomads, and exiles make up a great percentage of Biblical characters. God's people often immigrated, or migrated. Some of them moved because they were following God's command; others moved due to slavery or exile.

Adam and Eve were expelled from the Garden of Eden and "immigrated" to a new land. Cain, after murdering his brother, was expelled and sent to wander the earth as a fugitive exile. The first family lost their "citizenship" in Eden and had to find a new place to live.

Abraham immigrated to Canaan, and his nephew Lot immigrated to Sodom and Gomorrah. Later, Lot and his daughters immigrated again as they fled natural disaster and God's destruction of Sodom and Gomorrah.

The Old Testament list of immigrants is quite long. Some of the people were nomadic, others relocated and settled in foreign lands due to war or politics, and others were forced to relocate through slavery.

Here's a list of Old Testament immigrants: Noah, Naomi, Ruth, Rahab, countless slaves and concubines, captive children and youth such as Daniel, Shadrach, Meshach, Abednego, and

Esther. Jacob, his wives, and twelve sons immigrated more than once.

Moses was an immigrant. He fled from Egypt for refuge in Midian after killing an Egyptian. After years in Midian, he returned to Egypt to lead the children of Israel out of Egypt to the Promised Land of Canaan. The Israelites as a people left Egypt where they were enslaved and followed Moses—immigrating to Canaan.

The Bible continually reminds Israel that they were once slaves and immigrants. They were to remember where God brought them from as they lived in the Promised Land and interacted with "strangers." God commanded His people to love the strangers that lived among them.

Read Leviticus 19:34 and 25:23.

*But the **stranger** that dwelleth with you shall be unto you
as one born among you, and thou shalt love him as thyself;
for **ye were strangers** in the land of Egypt:
I am the LORD your God.*

*The land shall not be sold for ever: for the land is mine,
for **ye are strangers and sojourners** with me.*

Questions to Consider

1. What other Bible characters come to mind when you think of immigration?

2. Can you personally relate to immigration or relocation?

Chapter Five

Old Testament Treatment of Strangers

*But the **stranger** that dwelleth with you shall be unto you
as one born among you, and thou shalt love him as thyself;
for **ye were strangers** in the land of Egypt:
I am the LORD your God.*

Leviticus 19:34

Old Testament people faced unique problems in the immigration department, and there were clear guidelines on how to treat the strangers among the Israelites. I found two themes in the Old Testament when it came to interactions between Israel and the strangers. First, was the ethical and moral treatment of outsiders, and second, was the command to stay separate from ungodly foreign practices.

In over 45 verses, the Bible provides examples and commands concerning the ethical and moral treatment of immigrants and reminds Israel that they were once immigrants themselves. For each verse mentioned here, other verses addressed the same issues. Many of the commands concerned providing for the physical needs of immigrants.

Providing for Physical Needs

Read Leviticus 19:10.

And thou shalt not glean thy vineyard, neither shalt thou gather
every grape of thy vineyard; thou shalt leave them for the poor
*and **stranger**: I am the LORD your God.*

Here, God specifically orders the Israelites to purposefully leave food in their gardens so that the poor and "strangers" could have it. The story of Ruth is a perfect example of God's people providing for the physical needs of immigrants.

The story begins with Naomi and Elimelech immigrating away from Israel due to a famine. They traveled to the land of Moab where their two sons married Moabite women. Some years passed and Elimelech and his two sons died, leaving Naomi alone with two daughters-in-law. Naomi decided to return to Israel and told her daughters-in-law they were free to go back to their parent's houses.

One of the women decided to stay with Naomi; that woman's name was Ruth. They traveled back to Israel and where Ruth was considered a stranger in the land. Every day, Ruth would go out to the fields that belonged to the rich man, Boaz, and gather the leftover harvest after the servants had gleaned the fields. Boaz noticed Ruth and told his servants to purposefully leave good crops behind so that Ruth and Naomi would have food. At the conclusion of the story, Boaz marries Ruth.

There are many verses in which "strangers" are lumped together with the poor, fatherless (orphans) and widows. Throughout the Bible, we see examples of what would translate to the social programs of our day, to provide for those in need. We also see examples of individuals that took personal responsibility to care for the needy around them.

Read Deuteronomy 10:18.

> *He doth execute the judgment of the fatherless and widow,*
> *and loveth the **stranger**, in giving him food and raiment.*

Raiment means clothing. Here, the Bible is saying that it is right to give food and clothes to the fatherless, widows, and strangers (the immigrants)—the people that were in need, just like Naomi and Ruth.

Treating strangers, orphans, and widows well resulted in blessings from God.

Read Jeremiah 7:6.

> *If ye oppress not the **stranger**, the fatherless, and the widow,*
> *and shed not innocent blood in this place, neither walk after other*
> *gods to your hurt: then I will let you live in this place,*
> *in the land I gave your forefathers forever and ever.*

Questi♡ns t♡ C♡nsider

1. We just learned there are 45 scriptures that directly discuss the treatment of strangers or immigrants in the Bible. Can you remember any other Old Testament Biblical commands about how to treat immigrants?

2. How do the Old Testament Biblical principles concerning immigrants translate into our world today?

3. Besides providing for physical needs, what else can we do to help immigrants?

♥ Chapter Six ♥
Keep God First

Thou shalt have none other gods before me.

Deuteronomy 5:7

The second Old Testament theme on the treatment of strangers is the idea that taking up ungodly customs and cultures of immigrants could pull Israel away from God. Many verses attribute Israel's backsliding to the fact that people started worshipping foreign gods. Often, false gods were introduced after Israelite men married foreign wives. This theme is found particularly in Ezra 10:10-11.

And Ezra the priest stood up, and said unto them,
*Ye have transgressed, and have taken **strange** wives,*
to increase the trespass of Israel. Now therefore make confession
unto the LORD God of your fathers, and do his pleasure:
and separate yourselves from the people of the land,
*and from the **strange** wives.*

We see that Old Testament leaders often blamed foreign wives for problems. At times, the Israelite people were commanded to renounce their marriages to foreigners (Ezra 9 and 10, and Nehemiah 13).

Despite these instances, there are many more examples of another route to repent from worshiping foreign gods, rather than separating from "strange" spouses. There are several Biblical examples of Israelites who married foreigners and were blessed of God because they remained committed to serving Him.

Joseph married Asenath, the daughter of Potiphera (Genesis 41:45 and 50, and 46:20). Moses married an Ethiopian woman

(Numbers 12:1). Boaz married Ruth. Salmon married Rahab the war-spy (1 Chronicles 2:10-11, Ruth 4:20,21, Matthew 1:4-5 and Luke 3:32).

Clearly, Biblical commands warning against marrying strangers were issued solely for the protection of the spiritual practices of the people, and not meant as a rule against all international or multicultural marriages.

More often, it was the foreigner among the Israelites that had to separate themselves from their customs, culture, and gods. Many verses in the books of the law deal with what is required from the strangers living among the Israelites.

Exodus 12:49 is one example of the many times the Bible talks of having one law that is for both Israel and people from other nations.

One law shall be to him that is homeborn,
*and unto the **stranger** that sojourneth among you.*

Deuteronomy 5:14 says that the Sabbath day should be kept by both the children of Israel and the strangers.

But the seventh day is the sabbath of the LORD thy God:
in it thou shalt not do any work, thou, nor thy son, nor thy daughter,
nor thy manservant, nor thy maidservant, nor thine ox . . .
*nor thy **stranger** that is within thy gates; that thy manservant*
and thy maidservant may rest as well as thou.

Exodus 12:48 specifies that immigrants that adopted the religion of Israel were expected to participate in religious traditions.

*And when a **stranger** shall sojourn with thee,*
and will keep the passover to the LORD,
let all his males be circumcised, and then let him come near
and keep it; and he shall be as one that is born in the land:
for no uncircumcised person shall eat thereof.

Many immigrants left false gods and began following the one true God. Both Rahab and Ruth are great examples of such immigrants, and both were honored to be a part of the lineage of Jesus!

Questions to Consider

1. Think about the inter-cultural relationships you have. What can you learn from foreign customs?

2. What are some international customs you can participate in that do not conflict with serving God?

For example: wearing cultural clothing, celebrating holidays, learning or participating in a foreign physical exercise or discipline, learning a new language, or eating international foods.

3. Are there spiritual dangers in participating in some foreign traditions?

For example: spiritually revering foreign religious texts and giving them equal weight with the Bible, praying to false gods.

Chapter SEVEN

Love Your Neighbor

*Jesus said unto him, Thou shalt love the Lord thy God
with all thy heart, and with all thy soul, and with all thy mind.
This is the first and great commandment. And the second
is like unto it, Thou shalt love thy neighbor as thyself. On these two
commandments hang all the law and the prophets.*

Matthew 22:37-40

The New Testament also discusses God's plan for the way we treat immigrants. Traveling between nations was a big part of the culture in Jesus' time. Think about the stories of the good Samaritan, the Ethiopian ruler who was baptized in the desert, and the world-travelers who came to Jerusalem to celebrate Pentecost. Think about how common it was for the apostles to travel to new lands to evangelize. God often uses people's coming and going to increase His Kingdom.

In the gospel of Matthew, Jesus preaches to the disciples about judgment day. He makes it very clear we will be judged by the way we treat people who are in need, including the way we treat the immigrants around us.

The passage makes it clear: if we treat strangers with righteousness, it is as if we are treating Jesus with righteousness and we will be rewarded accordingly. If we treat strangers with evil, it is as if we are treating Jesus with evil, and we will be rewarded accordingly. We will be judged both on what we do and on what we neglect to do.

Read Matthew 25:21-46. Jesus is speaking of the day when He will return to earth and judge the world. Pay close attention to verses 35-40, and 42-45.

> *For I was an hungred, and ye gave me meat: I was thirsty, and ye gave me drink: **I was a stranger**, and ye took me in:*

Naked, and ye clothed me: I was sick, and ye visited me: I was in prison, and ye came unto me.

Then shall the righteous answer him, saying, Lord, when saw we thee an hungred, and fed thee? or thirsty, and gave thee drink?

*When saw we **thee a stranger**, and took thee in? or naked, and clothed thee?*

Or when saw we thee sick, or in prison, and came unto thee?

And the King shall answer and say unto them, Verily I say unto you, inasmuch as ye have done it unto one of the least of these my brethren, ye have done it unto me

*. . . For I was an hungred, and ye gave me no meat: I was thirsty, and ye gave me no drink: **I was a stranger**, and ye took me not in: naked, and ye clothed me not: sick, and in prison, and ye visited me not.*

*Then shall they also answer him, saying, Lord, when saw we thee an hungred, or athirst, **or a stranger**, or naked, or sick, or in prison, and did not minister unto thee?*

Then shall he answer them, saying, Verily I say unto you, inasmuch as ye did it not to one of the least of these, ye did it not to me.

Questions to Consider

1. When have you had the opportunity to meet the physical needs of someone else?

2. What can you do to proactively prepare to meet the needs of people you may meet?

For example, carry packed food items or restaurant gift cards in your car to give to the homeless. Volunteer to teach English to refugees. Invite foreign neighbors to social events to be sure they feel included and welcomed in the community. Spend time building friendships with international people, learning their stories, and sharing your stories.

Chapter Eight

A Spiritual Parallel

*Now therefore ye are no more **strangers and foreigners** . . .*

Ephesians 2:19

Why does the Bible mention immigrants so often? I believe it is for the practical application of how we are to treat people with human dignity and to help those in need, but I also believe there is a spiritual parallel that is important.

We need to remember where we came from (out of spiritual slavery to sin), and how God has brought us to the Promised Land (salvation). We need to remember the times when things were not going so well for us. We need to remember when others treated us poorly so that we will not treat others poorly.

Old Testament stories and references often foreshadowed things to come. I see the strangers or immigrants of the Old Testament as a representation of the believers in the New Testament.

Read Ephesians 2:12 and 19.

That at that time ye were without Christ,
*being **aliens** from the commonwealth of Israel,*
*and **strangers** from the covenants of promise,*
having no hope, and without God in the world . . .
*Now therefore ye are no more **strangers and foreigners**,*
*but **fellow citizens** with the saints,*
and of the household of God.

The spiritual parallel is clear: lost souls wander the world as travelers without a home. A lost soul can find citizenship in Christ and a homeland with believers. At the same time, believers are considered strangers in the world, traveling to the Promised Land—the heavenly home Jesus prepares for us.

Read 1 Peter 2:11.

> *Dearly beloved, I beseech you as **strangers and pilgrims** abstain from fleshly lusts, which war against the soul . . .*

In other words, keep yourself from the false gods, and ungodly ways and practices. We are to be "spiritual strangers" on earth.

Read Hebrews 11:8-10 and 13. Here believers are seen as wanderers on earth, seeking a *"city which has foundations, whose builder and maker is God."*

> *By faith Abraham, when he was called to go out into a place which he should after receive for an inheritance, obeyed; and he went out, **not knowing whither he went**.*
>
> *By faith he **sojourned** in the land of promise, as **in a strange country**, dwelling in tabernacles with Isaac and Jacob, the heirs with him of the same promise:*
>
> *For he looked for a city which hath foundations, whose builder and maker is God . . .*

*These all died in faith, not having received the promises, but having seen them afar off, and were persuaded of them, and embraced them, and confessed that they were **strangers and pilgrims** on the earth.*

Questions to Consider

1. How can you use your testimony as a Believer in Christ to relate to international immigrants living in your community?

2. As you reflect on your testimony, how does what Jesus has done for your life help foster compassion for immigrants?

3. How can you serve Christ by serving immigrant populations?

Chapter Nine

Ethics, Politics, & Humanitarian Efforts

Pure religion and undefiled before God and the Father is this,
To visit the fatherless and widows in their affliction,
and to keep himself unspotted from the world.

James 1:27

I would be in denial if I were to not mention the current political controversies in the U.S. concerning immigration. Many Christians choose to remain apolitical within a religious setting, a policy I agree with for the most part. At the same time, I believe the areas we are divided on as a nation need the light of God the most.

America—a country founded on immigrants, whether slave or free, colonizers or pilgrims—with her mixture of cultures and beliefs, is divided on current immigration issues. The descendants of immigrants argue about what to do with the millions of illegal immigrants in our country today. Believers who hold to Judeo-Christian values are on both sides of immigration politics.

My stance is that we as Christians have a duty and responsibility to consider the human soul first, and that meeting humanitarian needs with dignity and respect must be our priority.

I have friends in New Mexico that found themselves in trouble with the law for leaving water outside for people who were crossing into the country illegally. They had no interaction with the people crossing over; they simply left out water for them. My friends had to make a choice: allow human beings to possibly die of thirst, or be accused of aiding illegal immigrants. They chose to offer humanitarian aid in the form of water, despite whatever legal repercussions they faced.

Some other friends of mine once pastored a Spanish-speaking church. Many of the members of the church were afraid to give their full names, addresses, or to become involved because they were illegal immigrants. At times, some of the church people would not come to church because they were afraid of Immigration and Customs Enforcement (ICE) raids in their city.

Multicultural ministry requires a careful sensitivity to the people we minister to. Christians are called to focus on the needs of the human beings in front of us. Our question must be, "How can we be the hands and feet of Jesus?" We abide by the laws of the land, but we are not the police or ICE. We don't have to ask a person's immigration status to show them love and compassion, or to meet their basic human needs.

At the same time, there are, understandably, many Americans who feel very passionately about protecting their land and country. Some fear the financial burden of taking responsibility for the needs of illegal immigrants. If resources are used to help one people group, then there are no resources left to help others.

A simple tour of Ellis Island shows that Americans have always had some immigration concerns. Back when immigrants were all processed through the New York harbor, if a person was deemed to be a burden on society, unhealthy, or unable to bring something positive to the country, they were denied access and returned to their homelands.

This still happens at times. My mother, a nurse, told me the tragic story of one young man she cared for. He was an illegal immigrant who unfortunately was shot as a result of gang violence and left as a paraplegic. The hospital cared for him for a long time, but the young man had no way to pay for his care.

Eventually, it was decided that due to his illegal immigration status, he would be deported to his country. They gave him an electric wheelchair, put him on an airplane, and deposited him back to his hometown, a place without electricity or clean water. His story hurts my heart.

Some Americans may fear the cultural and political change that immigrants may bring. Throughout history, people groups have immigrated across lands, at times conquering local government powers and taking authority over new areas. Before the time of organized states and governments that we know of today, people often fought to defend their land from immigrants, and immigrants fought to conquer new lands.

Technically, the children of Israel were unwelcome, "illegal" immigrants who fought for and conquered the land God promised to them. Of course, the Bible does not distinguish between "legal" and "illegal" immigrants.

A poll conducted on Beliefnet.com found what Christians have to say about immigration. 61 percent said, "My faith teaches me to treat illegal immigrants as people in need of care and compassion." Another 24 percent said illegal immigrants are "lawbreakers who should be punished." And, 15 percent said illegal immigrants are "lawbreakers who should be forgiven."

From what we have already viewed about the Bible and immigration, it is obvious where those compassionate toward immigrants find their Biblical inspiration, but what about the 24 percent of believers that say that illegal immigrants are "lawbreakers who should be punished"? What scriptures do they base their thoughts on? There are verses that teach us to obey the laws of the land.

Read 1 Peter 2:13-14.

Submit yourselves to every ordinance of man for the Lord's sake:
whether it be to the king, as supreme; Or unto governors,
as unto them that are sent by him for the punishment of evildoers, and
for the praise of them that do well.

Read Romans 13:1 and 7.

Let every soul be subject unto the higher powers. For there is no power
but of God: the powers that be are ordained of God . . .
Render therefore to all their dues: tribute to whom tribute
is due; custom to whom custom; fear to whom fear;
honour to whom honour.

Read Titus 3:1-2.

Put them in mind to be subject to principalities and powers,
to obey magistrates, to be ready to every good work,
to speak evil of no man, to be no brawlers,
but gentle, shewing all meekness unto all men.

Over one million people immigrate to the United States each year, and there are currently over 40 million people living in the United States who were born in another country. Many immigrants are refugees fleeing for their lives and seeking a life where they can be safe. Every day, 5,000 children worldwide become refugees.

Current 2020 U.S. immigration policy allows for 18,000 immigrants with refugee status to enter the United States; the lowest number admitted since the creation of refugee resettlement program in 1980. Previous years' refugee admission numbers ranged from 30,000 to 80,000 refugees per year. Moving to a new country, learning a new language, finding new ways to bring in financial support, and building a new life is one of the most stressful and difficult undertakings a person can experience. Half of all immigrants live in three states: California, Texas, and New York.

Today, we have the opportunity to play a part in the lives and stories of immigrants. Supporting immigrants through the assimilation process ensures they have the resources to become productive and upstanding citizens. We can teach American values of freedom, respect, hard work, education, and compassion. Spiritually, we can shine the light of Christ into the lives of people who may never have had the opportunity to know the love and power of God before.

Many Americans, even some conservative Christians, struggle with fear of national security concerns, and sometimes even blatant prejudice. I think it is important to educate on the screening processes refuges go through to even come to the U.S. The process takes 18-24 months, and individuals go through many interviews for security and health screenings to vet them for entrance to the United States.

Fear of refugees being a national security risk is not supported by data, as only a fraction of refugees are arrested for terrorism-related charges. The United States is very strict when it comes to allowing people to immigrate if they have ever been connected to terror groups. Even victims who were violently forced to support terror groups are not allowed entrance into the U.S.

For example, a man who was kidnapped by a terror group and forced to cook and do other tasks for the group was denied entrance. A woman who was forced to provide food and supplies to a terror group was denied entrance, even though the same group destroyed her business once they were finished using it. Victims who were forced to pay ransoms to free themselves or their relatives from terror groups are denied entrance to the United States. Too often victims are treated like criminals, barred from finding a safe place to live—and some of them resort to illegal immigration to live in safety.

During every generation, believers have had to make ethical and moral choices on how they would live out their faith in the middle of their society and current world politics. It's a personal choice each of us must make. I have decided that if the laws of the land conflict with my faith, I will stand on the Word of God.

As ministers of the Gospel, our job is to love people. We are called to love, to pray, and to provide a service that offers an atmosphere of worship where people can come and make a connection with God. Maybe God has gifted us with being able to offer other services as well, like an English class, or a citizenship class, a food bank, a clothing or school supply drive, or some other kind of social support. As Christians, these are the ways we often serve the immigrants around us.

American Christians have a unique and beautiful opportunity to minister to the entire world right from their hometowns. We have the resources to make a worldwide difference, and we use those resources to make our world a better place. Our country is known for the way we give financially to humanitarian causes around the world.

It is my prayer that Christians would rise up to love the immigrants in their communities, to actively participate in the assimilation process, to embrace international people and to welcome them into friendships, families, and church communities.

Questi♥ns t♥ C♥nsider

1. How does God call us to treat the immigrants among us? What about international people who are in need in foreign lands?

2. Why do some people fear immigrants?

3. Does God's call for our behavior toward others change depending on another's circumstance?

For example, what if an immigrant is from a country that has a negative political history with our country? Or what if the immigrant's legal status is unclear?

♡ Chapter Ten ♡

Dear to Us

But we were gentle among you, like a nursing mother taking care of her own children. So being affectionately desirous of you, we were ready to share with you not only the gospel of God but also our own selves, because you had become very dear to us.

1 Thessalonians 1:7-8 ESV

My heart has been torn for the refugees and immigrants forced to leave their homes due to ISIS and other incredibly evil groups. Some of the refugees are right here where I currently live in San Antonio.

I was told there are around 70,000 Middle Easterners in the city. I meet them often—in restaurants, driving my Ubers, towing my car. They are from all over, but I often find myself connecting with people from Iraq—not even knowing they are from Iraq until after we begin engaging in conversations.

I remember watching the news in the 2015 time frame—when the ISIS beheadings were the main story. I turned off the TV, went to my bedroom, got on my knees and cried. I couldn't stop crying. My heart broke for the Yazidi people, the Kurds, the Muslims, and the Christians—everyone facing persecution.

I have since learned that there are many children, abandoned, poor and often starving on the streets in Iraq. These children were born as a result of ISIS rapes, so people call them demon children. Current laws prevent non-Muslims from adopting these orphans. My heart is with those children.

Many people in Iraq do not have much to give away to help others. For months, people have been protesting government corruption and hoping to gain the attention of U.S. intervention. They want jobs and opportunities. They want oppression to stop. One of my friends has family involved in the protests. I have seen many of their videos posted on Facebook. As I write,

U.S. troops are on their way to Baghdad after the recent Iranian-based attack on the U.S. embassy there.

I don't know where Jesus will take me in the future, but I do know that the first part of my life has led me to compassion. One day, I pray I see an international revival here in America.

Maybe I will be involved in a multicultural church that sends humanitarian aid to help people in their home countries. Maybe I will have an opportunity to adopt a child from overseas. But for now, I only have myself, my time, my life, and my heart to give. Thankfully, that is all Jesus needs. His plan is so much bigger than ours, and His grace is sufficient.

When I read 1 Thessalonians 1:7-8, I can't help but think about how Paul, once a Middle Eastern terrorist, became one of the greatest evangelists of all time. He went to the nations and people others rejected. He loved people and he made an impact. I am not Paul, but I have something in me that resonates with who he was and the message he preached. Jesus. The Lord's compassion never fails, and His love and mercy endure forever.

I'd like to share the story of a woman I know from Kurdistan, Iraq. We sat in a classroom alone for over an hour as we worked through her story as she prepared to share her experiences at a local library event. We cried together. We prayed together. We talked and dreamed about ways we could make a difference together.

She apologized for making me cry.

"Why are you apologizing?" I asked. "I need to cry. It is the least that I can do when the people of your country are suffering the way they are. I hope every person who hears your story cries. Maybe it will move them to do something to make a difference."

The following story is what we prepared for her to share, so it's written from her perspective. She gave me permission to use it in this book.

♡

I am from Kurdistan, Iraq. I came to America in 2011, nine years ago. I am here with my husband and my three daughters. My mother lives with my two brothers in Michigan.

My family and I came to America because our country was not safe. There were kidnappings, bombings, murder, and no jobs. It was not a good life.

When you go outside to go shopping, or to do anything, you never say, "I'll be back" because you don't know that you will be back. You might die.

My cousin went shopping for clothes for her young son. She never came back. There was a bomb. Her husband went to look for her, but her body was destroyed. All he could find was her hand. There was nothing left of their son.

Some days, when I am at home alone, I cry when I think of my memories and what I've seen with the people there in my country. Over there, they will steal children and ask for money. They say if you don't bring the money the next day, they will kill the children.

Many people there have nothing. They don't have good food. They don't have medicine. The food and medicine that come from Iran are sometimes bad. Once they gave shots to help with sicknesses, but the shots gave the people AIDS.

I know of a family that is in Iraq. The father and the sons were killed—only the mother and her three daughters were left. They had no food. The mother became sick in her mind, and she killed herself. Now the daughters are left with no one.

Many children do not have a mom or a dad. Their families were killed. Why were they killed? Not for religion, but for power.

So many people die there. So many people kill themselves because they have nothing. No jobs. No future. They have troubled minds. I don't know if my country will ever have a good future.

I have a sister there still in Iraq. She is not safe. There are many ISIS members around who do not like Kurdish people. My sister keeps a bag with her IDs and passports ready to go. She sleeps with her car key in her hand. She is ready to leave at any time to take her family to another city.

When I left Iraq, I asked my sister to come with me, but her husband's parents were elderly, and they could not leave them behind. Her husband's father is in a wheelchair with no legs. My sister said she could not leave her husband and his parents. They are like her parents.

When I first left Iraq, I went to Turkey and then to the United States. I was excited to come to the U.S., but also nervous. I did not speak any English. I didn't know how people would react to me wearing a hijab.

But now I am okay. No one has ever bullied me. Some people see my hijab and come up to me and say, "I love you." I feel accepted here. I love it.

In my country, I never went to school. Now, I am speaking and reading English. It's a good life. I love America. I am now a citizen.

I do what I can to help the people in my country. If I can send $100 it can feed many families. Even if I can send $10, it can feed at least one family.

We all can pray. I pray for peace every day, for every country, and every person. We all can make a difference.

♥

This next story is from another woman I volunteered with. We prepared her story for the library presentation as well. She is from Chad, Africa, and gave me permission to share her story.

♡

I have been in America for ten years. I became a citizen on August 15, 2017. I came to America with my children. We had to leave because of the war in my country.

The current president of Chad overthrew the previous president. The old president was a Christian, and the new President is a Muslim that does not like all people. He said he would kill all of the Christians in Chad.

I and my family are Christians. The president sent soldiers to our village to kill everyone. That day, I was sick and at the hospital, and had my young children with me, so I was able to escape.

My husband understood what the soldiers were saying in Arabic and translated for my son. My husband told my son the soldiers said they were going to kill everyone after their prayers. My son and daughter were able to get away, but the soldiers captured my husband and most of the people in our village.

They put my husband in jail, and they killed everyone else, leaving their bodies out for the animals. After five months, they killed my husband too.

I took my children and went from the hospital to a refugee camp in Cameroon, Africa, a neighboring country on the boarder of Chad. At the refugee camp, they said they could not help me because I was from Chad. Many people from Cameroon do not like people from Chad. They left us outside with no food or water. It took two years before I was able to find my oldest son and daughter again.

War is no good. I cannot go back to my country. I would have died a long time ago if I was in Africa. I am scared to go back with the president that is there. They have pictures of me and my children and will kill us if we were to return.

I am so thankful to be in America with my children. I am the only child left from my parents. I have no aunts, uncles, or other family besides my children and now my grandchildren.

All of my children have gone to school in America. Now they have jobs and do their best. It can still be a struggle. I receive disability and do the best I can.

At Thanksgiving, someone gave my family a meal and I am so grateful. At times, we are low on money and do not have food. I have some of my grandchildren that live with me.

Please pray for me and my family that we can continue living for God. God has blessed me and takes care of me and my children.

♥

Other nations face harsh realities. Sometimes, we hide from thinking about what goes on in the world because we don't want to hear about tragedy. But that doesn't change the truth about what real people are facing all over the world. They bring their stories and experiences with them when they immigrate.

There are so many more stories I wish I could share, and maybe I will one day. For now, I am honored that I could share my heart for "my strangers" in this simple way.

Thank you for taking the time to read, to reflect, and to think about what you can do to make a difference. God is calling us to love each other, to care, and to do what we can to help. How can you help the people in your world? What will you do to become involved, to show kindness, or to build a friendship? You can change a life and the world.

Our world needs love and we can make a difference. What if you were to connect to local immigrants and learn their stories? It's a small step, but it can make a big difference.

I believe loving these people who live among us, and learning about them will spur us to action. We can fight world hunger, provide water for the thirsty, adopt and care for orphans, fight human trafficking, and stop cultural annihilation—in short, we can fight evil in the world today. We may not be able to do it all, but each individual can do something, and collectively we can do even more.

We can all pray and there is much power in prayer. Communicate with God. Stop talking and start listening to what He is saying. He will direct your steps and lead you to do exactly what He wants you to do. It starts with a love for the strangers.

Refugee Assimilation Initiative

I wrote the following research paper for a college class I attended at Texas Bible College. I used a small part of this paper in an earlier chapter, but wanted to include the entire work here.

Our country is full of beautiful immigration stories. Over one million people immigrate to the United States each year, and there are currently over 40 million people living in the United States who were born in another country (Radford, 2019). Many immigrants are refugees fleeing for their lives and seeking a life where they can be safe. Every day, 5,000 children worldwide become refugees (Fantino & Colack, 2001).

Justification

Current U.S. immigration policy for 2020 allows for 18,000 immigrants with refugee status enter the United States; the lowest number admitted since the creation of refugee resettlement program in 1980 (Krogstad, 2019). Previous years' refugee admission numbers ranged from 30,000 to 80,000 refugees per year (Krogstad, 2019). Moving to a new country, learning a new language, finding new ways to bring in financial support, and building a new life is one of the most stressful and difficult undertakings a person can experience. Half of all immigrants live in three states: California, Texas, and New York (Radford, 2019). "More than 3 million refugees have resettled in their new homes in the U.S. since 1975, making the U.S. the top resettlement country in the world. In 2016, Texas received the second highest number of U.S.-bound refugees [7,802] after California [7,909], as the U.S. welcomed 84,994 refugees. Specifically, Bexar County, which includes San Antonio, hosted more than 1,000 refugees" (Adel, 2019).

Description of target population, stakeholders, & participants

The aim of this project is to provide a consultation program to educate local organizations on the need for assimilation support, to identify an area of support that each willing local organization can provide, and to build a network of resources that share a common goal—supporting the immigrant in assimilating to life in America. Target organizations include educational institutions, religious organizations, and social clubs and programs. These stakeholders and participants are already serving their communities providing various services and can easily extend special help to support the assimilation process in a professional manner.

Description of how project will influence social change

Today, we have the opportunity to play a part in the lives and stories of immigrants. Supporting immigrants through the assimilation process ensures they have the resources to become productive and upstanding citizens. We can teach American values of freedom, respect, hard work, education, and compassion. Spiritually, we can shine the light of Christ into the lives of people who may never have had the opportunity to know the love and power of God before. The spiritual component is the most important, as knowing God can positively impact generations of families to come.

Data collection and methods to analyze needs

It's important to identify the immigrant population, and their needs in the local community, as this will vary from place to place. Working together with government officials, refugee resettlement programs, and public education systems who have already identified needs can save time and resources. Even more importantly is including refugee voices in the planning process and asking them what they need (Ives, 2007). Some needs or issues may include:

Culture shock, understanding norms, customs, laws, and acceptable behavior in the foreign environment. This need will be greater for people groups moving to cultures very different from their own. For example, an Iraqi family moving to the U.S. will face a greater challenge than they would moving to Syria, Jordan, or returning to their homeland after turmoil has calmed (Masterson, 2010).

Financial assistance/material needs. Many refuges are resettled with financial assistance well below the poverty line. The U.S. Government purchases plane tickets for refugee families, which is then due as a no-interest loan. For large families, this may mean $10,000 or $20,000 of debt (Masterson, 2010). They are typically given an apartment or house with furniture, food, and a one-time payment of $450, 80 days of free health insurance, and 30-90 days of assistance in finding a job, scheduling medical appointments, and enrolling in school (Masterson, 2010).

Language learning and employment. These are the two greatest needs of refuges (Masterson, 2010). This is a challenge for both educated and uneducated people. With the economic crisis, less than 50 percent of refuges find jobs within six months of resettlement (Masterson, 2010).

Mental and emotional health support. Often refugees have been victims of terror and abuse on a number of levels. They may experience PTSD and lasting effects from trauma that may impact their cognitive and daily functioning (Kaplan, 2009). Service providers should be aware of potential histories of refugee immigrants and be equipped to treat them with respect as victims who have experienced human rights violations (Kaplan, 2009).

Analysis of evidence-based research related to the interventions

There are many ways organizations, professionals, and individuals can support the refugee assimilation initiative. Providing for material and physical needs, such as offering free health clinics, delivering food bank packages, or offering free haircuts can all be a benefit. Individuals can put forth an effort to building relationships, show kindness, and be neighborly. They can invite refugees to their homes to share a meal, include them in social gatherings, and encourage friendship between their children and refugee children. There is no limit to the ways we can help the assimilation process. All that is required is a compassionate heart, and a little bit of creativity. The following are examples of ways to support the refugee assimilation process.

Story Telling, Listening, and Honoring Experiences. The simple act of sharing stories and relating to common human experiences can form bonds that transcend culture and build unity. Preserving family histories and acknowledging the experience of refugees can improve acceptance in educational and social circles (Roy, 2015). Often, U.S. refugee programs focus on equipping the person to be financially self-sufficient so they are not dependent on the government for support, but these programs do not take into consideration the heart of the person and their needs for connecting in community while preserving a sense of cultural integrity (Ives, 2007).

Mental Health First Aid Training. Educating the refugee community on recognizing depression, anxiety, and other mental health challenges has led to significant improvement in recognizing symptoms and professional treatment options (Subedi et al., 2015).

Language Learning. Language is the key to participating in social, cultural, and political life (Atwell, Gifford, & McDonald-Wilmsen, 2009). Refugees and immigrants may experience struggle in spending time looking for a job or working, and spending time learning a language. In some cultures, women may have never been exposed to educational opportunities in the past and may not feel motivated to learn a new language if they are primarily at home.

Understanding the local refugee population can provide untraditional language opportunities. For example, some populations may already have the foundation to communicate in Spanish more easily than in English. Roy (2015) found Somli families integrated more easily into Latino culture and frequently used Spanish at home. Offering English classes and childcare at local apartment complexes where refugees live may encourage women to participate. Atwell, Gifford, & McDonald-Wilmsen (2009) found that refugee parents who learned a new language were better able to communicate with their children who learn the language and culture at school and are less likely to engage in severe physical abuse.

Job Placement and Creation. Refugees have a variety of experiences, skill sets, and abilities that can be strategically used in the community when they are recognized (Buscher, 2011). Refugees are a source of skilled labor who are very resilient, willing to work, and committed to positive work ethic. Communities can aid in job placement and creation when organizations commit to hiring refugees. For example, a hospital in San Antonio is working with a local Christian ministry that outreaches to the refugee community to create food service and janitorial jobs specifically for people who lack language skills.

Free Medical and Dental Care Clinics. Medical professionals can offer medical and dental care clinics based at community locations on specific days each month.

Free services. In the same way, hairstylists, resume writers, tutors, teachers, food banks, and many other people who provide services can volunteer at select locations monthly. Services could be advertised to refugee communities in need.

Child Specific Outreach. Refugee children face not only the normal difficulties all children face growing up, but also the traumas that led them to immigrate with their families, cultural conflict between home and school, and sometimes prejudice and racism (Fantino & Colak, 2001). Providing free child-friendly activities, local summer camps, fine arts opportunities, and other venues to connect to locals through clubs and mentorship programs can build relationships, offer opportunities for healing and growth, and influence future generations.

Explanation of the project goals and how to assess them

The main goals of this project are to educate local organizations, secure buy-in and participation in the refugee assimilation process, and to build a community and network to serve this population. Assessment of the goals would belong to the administrative leader of the initiative. Assessment would include projected growth of the program, the number of presentations given yearly, participation of local organizations, fund-raising, and communication to partners via social media, newsletters, meetings, and sharing statistics.

An action plan, including tasks to be implemented

The administrative person or team would be responsible for scheduling and giving presentations, planning monthly or quarterly community partner meetings, following up with local organizations, collecting data from participating organizations, celebrating achievements, and telling success stories. It may also include some political activism and educating community members on current policies and laws.

Possible challenges and how they may be addressed

Many Americans, even conservative Christians who should be approaching others with compassion and empathy first, struggle with fears of national security concerns, or even with blatant prejudice. This can be a source of internal challenge that keeps communities from embracing foreigners. It is important to educate Americans on the screening processes refuges go through to even come to the U.S. The process takes 18-24 months, and individuals go through many interviews for security and health screenings to vet them for entrance to the United States (Knight, 2017).

Fear of refugees being a national security risk is not supported by data, as only a fraction of refugees are arrested for terrorism-related charges (Knight, 2017). Even victims who are violently forced to support terror groups are not allowed entrance into the U.S.

For example, a man who was kidnapped by a terror group and forced to cook and do other tasks for the group was denied entrance (Knight, 2017). A woman who was forced to provide food and supplies to a terror group, who's businesses were later destroyed by the same group despite her obedience was denied entrance (Knight, 2017). Victims who are forced to pay ransoms to free themselves or their relatives from terror groups are denied entrance to the United States (Martin & Ferris, 2017). Too often victims are treated like criminals, barred from finding a safe place to live—so they often resort to illegal immigration.

If these statistics are not enough to ease the fears of locals, it makes sense from a national security standpoint, that we ensure immigrants are supported in the assimilation process, so we can prevent national security disasters by providing mental health support, education, material resources, job security, and social acceptance and integration into society.

References

Adel, Fadi (2019). San Antonio refugees: Their demographics, healthcare profiles, and how to better serve them. PLoS One. https://www.ncbi.nlm.nih.gov/pmc/articles/PMC6380579

Atwell, R., Gifford, S. M., & McDonald-Wilmsen, B. (2009). Resettled Refugee Families and Their Children's Futures: Coherence, Hope and Support. Journal of Comparative Family Studies, 40(5), 677–697.

Buscher, D. (2011). New Approaches to Urban Refugee Livelihoods. Refuge (0229-5113), 28(2), 17–29.

Ives, N. (2007). More than a "Good Back": Looking for Integration in Refugee Resettlement. Refuge (0229-5113), 24(2), 54–63.

Fantino, A. M., & Colak, A. (2001). Refugee Children in Canada: Searching for Identity. Child Welfare, 80(5), 587–596.

Kaplan, I. (2009). Effects of trauma and the refugee experience on psychological assessment processes and interpretation. Australian Psychologist, 44(1), 6–15.

Knight, K. (2017). U.S. refugee exclusion practices. Forced Migration Review, 54, 52–53.

Krogstad, J. (2019, October 7). Key facts about refugees to the U.S. Pew Research Center. https://www.pewresearch.org/fact-tank/2019/10/07/key-facts-about-refugees-to-the-u-s/

Martin, S. F., & Ferris, E. (2017). U.S. Leadership and the International Refugee Regime. Refuge (0229-5113), 33(1), 18–28.

Masterson, D. (2010). An American Dream: The Broken Iraqi Refugee Resettlement Program and How to Fix It. Harvard Kennedy School Review, 10, 4–7.

Radford, J. (2019, June 17). Key findings about U.S. immigrants. Pew Research Center. www.pewresearch.org/fact-tank/2019/06/17/key-findings-about-u-s-immigrants

Roy, L. A. (2015). Borders and Intersections of Possibility: Multilingual Repertoires of Refugee Families in the Southwest U.S. Multicultural Perspectives, 17(2), 61–68.

Subedi, P., Changwei Li, Gurung, A., Bizune, D., Dogbey, M. C., Johnson, C. C., & Yun, K. (2015). Mental health first aid training for the Bhutanese refugee community in the United States. International Journal of Mental Health Systems, 9(1), 1–7.

Rachael Kathleen Hartman

Hi, I'm Rachael, the owner of Our Written Lives, LLC, a Christian publishing company I started in 2012.

My writing career began in college when I worked for the student newspaper, *The Inkwell,* and as a freelancer for *The Spirit Newspapers* in Bloomingdale, Georgia.

In graduate school, I started editing doctoral dissertations through a website I started called *The Grammar Queen Editorial Consulting and Writing Services.* After that, I worked as a full-time newspaper reporter at *The Hardin County News,* a branch of *The Beaumont Enterprise,* in Lumberton, Texas.

Around 2014, I started freelance writing religious education curriculum for middle school, high school, and college-aged students through Word Aflame Press, P7 Bible Clubs, and Link247.

I have a Master of Science degree in Human Services with a Specialization in Counseling from Capella University, and a Bachelor of Arts in Liberal Studies with a Minor in Writing from Armstrong Atlantic State University.

I'm happy to say that I'm currently completing a Bachelor's degree in Christian Ministry at Texas Bible College, which I originally started nearly 20 years ago.

Books by Rachael Kathleen Hartman:

- *Angel: The True Story of an Undeserved Chance (2013)*
- *Called to Write Chosen to Publish:*
    Inspiration for Christian Authors (2015)
- *Facing Myself: An Introspective Look at Cosmetic Surgery (2016)*
- *Llamada a Escribir, Elegida a Publicar (2018)*
- *A Love for the Strangers:*
    What the Bible Says About Loving Immigrants (2021)

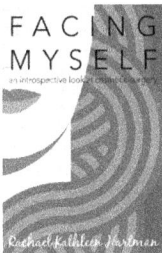

♥

Our Written Lives
book publishing services

www.ingramcontent.com/pod-product-compliance
Lightning Source LLC
Chambersburg PA
CBHW070028030426
42335CB00017B/2334